The Adventures of Ryan and Rachel

When Ryan met Rachel

Written By
LaShawn Marshall

Illustrated By
Abira Das

ISBN: 0692667520
ISBN 13: 9780692667521

To Ryan and Rachel my true adventurers
Thank you for letting me share your story
Love Mommy.

"Mommy!" Ryan called out running into the living room "Can you please explain to Rachel how we met?" Their mommy put the book she was reading down "why?" She asked and before Ryan could tell her Rachel ran in the room crying "Ryan said that you and daddy found me in the park when I was one year old and nobody wanted me so you brought me home!" Rachel crawled onto her mother's lap sniffling.

Their mommy looked at Ryan with disapproval, Ryan gave a sad look and shrugged his shoulders. "Ryan why would you tell your sister something like that?" Their mommy asked "She had my toy and she made me mad" he answered.

Their Mother patted the seat on the couch next to her for him to sit down "just because someone makes you unhappy does not mean you say hurtful things to them, you let them know how you feel and then they will stop and if they don't you walk away". "Okay, sorry Rachel" Ryan said feeling sad that he hurt his little sister's feelings "it's okay Ryan" Rachel said wiping the tears from her eyes.

7

"Mommy I tried to fix it but now she won't believe me, can you please tell her how we met" Ryan asked looking up at his mother with tears in his eyes. "Yes, I will tell the story of how you two met". She said wiping his eyes. "Tell her the way you told my class, that makes it more interesting, Rachel you're going to love it mommy tells it just like a real story, but it's all true" Ryan said excitedly.

9

When Ryan was three years old his father and I brought home a little surprise for him. I sat down in the rocking chair and called Ryan over. Hugging him I said "Ryan, I have someone I would like for you to meet" Ryan looked up at me and asked "who?" At that moment his father brought over what looked like a little chair filled with blankets.

"I would like you to meet your new baby sister, Rachel" I said. Ryan examined the blankets and frowned "what baby sister, it's just a bunch of blankets" and then the blankets moved and made a sound, Ryan opened his eyes in shock. His father pulled the blankets away and sitting there with her eyes wide open was Rachel.

"Hey there's a baby in there!" Ryan yelled, this scared Rachel and she started to cry. Ryan jumped after hearing the noise and covered his ears "why is she making that noise?" He asked. "Babies aren't use to loud noises they get scared easily so, we have to always make sure we are quiet when they are around" his father said while calming Rachel down.

Ryan slipped out of my arms to get a closer look of his new baby sister. As Ryan got closer Rachel opened her eyes and looked at him "hi Rachel" Ryan said touching the little hand that was sticking out. His father reminded him that he had to be gentle with Rachel so she doesn't get hurt. "Daddy?" Ryan called while he was still looking Rachel over "yes Ryan?" "Can you take her back to the hospital and get a boy?"

"Sorry son she's ours to keep, why do you want a boy?" His father asked. Ryan watched as I took Rachel out of the seat with all the blankets. Rachel was so small to him he thought she looked like a toy. "Because she's so small she can't play with me" "Don't worry when Rachel gets bigger she will be able to play with you" I said. "How long is that going to take?" Ryan was not convinced that, that little thing in his mommy's arms was ever going to get big enough to play with him.

Throughout the day Ryan watched as his Mommy and Daddy took care of this little baby that will be staying with them. He saw us feed her, change her, and talk to her. He didn't understand why we were talking to her because she never talked back. When Rachel went to sleep his father played quiet games with Ryan so I could get some rest as well.

Ryan liked playing with his father but he wasn't used to playing quiet games and he wasn't sure yet how he felt about it. He still didn't believe that Rachel would be any fun to play with because all she did right now was sleep, and where was the fun in that?

At bed time I told Ryan a bed time story about a big brother named Ryan who would go on adventures with his little sister Rachel. I told him about how Ryan would help Rachel and teach her things that only big brothers can teach like how to play soccer and catch.

The more Ryan listened to me the more excited he became. He couldn't wait to get up the next day and start teaching Rachel things. "Mommy I am going to be the best big brother ever" Ryan said while I tucked him in "I know you are sweetie, now get some sleep". I gave him a kiss on the forehead and turned off his light.

The next morning Ryan woke up bright and early and he went into Rachel's room. He pulled up his stool that was next to her crib and peeked in on her, he was surprise to see she was up and looking at him. "Good morning" he said to her. "My name is Ryan, I am your big brother and I am here to teach you."

Rachel started to scrunch up her face and let out a loud cry "Ryan jumped down off the stool and ran to my room "mommy, mommy! Rachel doesn't want me to teach her anything, I told her I was there to teach her and she started to yell at me" Ryan said with a worried look on his face. "Ryan, she wasn't yelling at you she's just crying, she's probably hungry." I said "Babies can't talk so they sometimes cry to let people know they need something. She saw you and was trying to tell you to come and get me."

"Oh" Ryan said as he followed me back to his sister's room and watched as I calmed her down. "Ryan can you be a great big brother and keep an eye on Rachel while I go get her milk?" Ryan was scared but he felt proud that I trusted him with such an important job "sure mommy, I'll watch her" he said standing back up on the stool. He stood there staring at Rachel staring at him "let's have a stare contest" he told her remembering that, that was one of the quiet games he played with his father the day before.

By the time I came back he already played four rounds with his sister "mommy I have to teach Rachel how to play the stare game she keeps blinking" "maybe when she gets a little bigger" I said "here would you like to help me feed her?" Ryan agreed and listened as I showed him how to hold the bottle and feed Rachel while I held her.

Ryan felt very good to be able to help me, just then his father came in the room and gave him a high five for being such a great big brother. "Maybe this big brother thing won't be so bad after all" Ryan said to his father as he continued to help me.

I laid Rachel back down in her crib Ryan stepped up on his stool and reached out to touch her hand "we are going to have some great adventures together" he said to her as she grabbed his finger, and that is how Ryan met Rachel. Their mommy said pinching Rachel's nose.

39

Feeling better Rachel got down off their mother's lap "mommy is that really how Ryan and I met?" "Yes sweetie" Rachel smiled "I like that story it's now my favorite." She turned to Ryan and said "I'm sorry I made you mad Ryan" "and I'm sorry I made you sad" Ryan said hugging Rachel "you're the best little sister ever, and I'm happy daddy didn't take you back to the hospital and change you for a boy."

Meet Ryan & Rachel!

A brother and sister who love to go on adventures together.
This adventure is about how they met and Ryan coming
to terms with being a big brother.

www.ingramcontent.com/pod-product-compliance
Lightning Source LLC
Chambersburg PA
CBHW041546040426
42447CB00002B/61